CHINESE
HOROSCOPES
FOR
LOVERS

The Dog

LORI REID

illustrated by
PAUL COLLICUTT

ELEMENT BOOKS

Shaftesbury, Dorset • Rockport, Massachusetts • Brisbane, Queensland

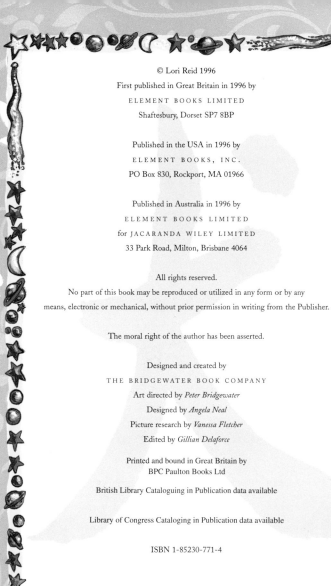

© Lori Reid 1996

First published in Great Britain in 1996 by

ELEMENT BOOKS LIMITED

Shaftesbury, Dorset SP7 8BP

Published in the USA in 1996 by

ELEMENT BOOKS, INC.

PO Box 830, Rockport, MA 01966

Published in Australia in 1996 by

ELEMENT BOOKS LIMITED

for JACARANDA WILEY LIMITED

33 Park Road, Milton, Brisbane 4064

Designed and created by

THE BRIDGEWATER BOOK COMPANY

Art directed by *Peter Bridgewater*

Designed by *Angela Neal*

Picture research by *Vanessa Fletcher*

Edited by *Gillian Delaforce*

Printed and bound in Great Britain by
BPC Paulton Books Ltd

British Library Cataloguing in Publication data available

Library of Congress Cataloging in Publication data available

ISBN 1-85230-771-4

Contents

犬

8

Why are some people lucky in love and others not?

Chinese Astrology

SOME PEOPLE fall in love and, as the fairy tales go, live happily ever after. Others fall in love – again and again, make the same mistakes every time and never form a lasting relationship. Most of us come between these two extremes, and

some people form remarkably successful unions while others make spectacular disasters of their personal lives. Why are some people lucky in love while others have the odds stacked against them?

ANIMAL NAMES

According to the philosophy of the Far East, luck has very little to do with it. The answer, the philosophers say, lies with 'the Animal that hides in our hearts'. This Animal, of which there are 12, forms part of the complex art of Chinese Astrology. Each year of a 12-year cycle is attributed an Animal sign, whose characteristics are said to influence worldly events as well as the personality and fate of each living thing that comes under its dominion. The 12 Animals run in sequence, beginning with the Rat and followed by the Ox, Tiger, Rabbit, Dragon, Snake, Horse, Sheep, Monkey, Rooster, Dog and last, but not least, the Pig. Being born in the Year of the Ox, for example, is simply a way of describing what you're like, physically and psychologically. And this is quite different from someone who, for instance, is born in the Year of the Snake.

犬

9

*The 12
Animals
of Chinese
Astrology.*

RELATIONSHIPS

These Animal names are merely the tip of the ice-berg, considering the complexity of the whole subject. Yet such are the richness and wisdom of Chinese Astrology that understanding the principles behind the year in which you were born will give you powerful insights into your own personality. The system is very specific about which Animals are compatible and which are antagonistic and this tells us whether our relationships will be successful. Marriages are made in heaven, so the saying goes. The heavens, according to Chinese beliefs, can point the way. The rest is up to us.

犬

10

Year Chart and Birth Dates

UNLIKE THE WESTERN CALENDAR, which is based on the Sun, the Oriental year is based on the movement of the Moon, which means that New Year's Day does not fall on a fixed date. This Year Chart, taken from the Chinese Perpetual Calendar, lists the dates on which each year begins and ends together with its Animal ruler for the year. In addition, the Chinese believe that the tangible world is composed of 5 elements, each slightly adapting the characteristics of the Animal signs. These elemental influences are also given here. Finally, the aspect, that is, whether the year is characteristically Yin (-) or Yang (+), is also listed.

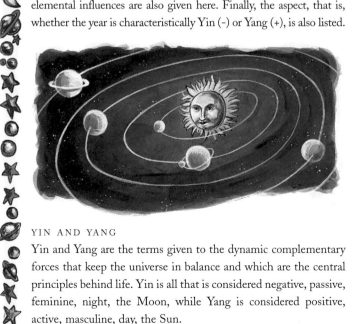

The Western calendar is based on the Sun; the Oriental on the Moon.

YIN AND YANG

Yin and Yang are the terms given to the dynamic complementary forces that keep the universe in balance and which are the central principles behind life. Yin is all that is considered negative, passive, feminine, night, the Moon, while Yang is considered positive, active, masculine, day, the Sun.

犬

Year	From – To	Animal sign	Element	Aspect
1900	31 Jan 1900 – 18 Feb 1901	Rat	Metal	+ Yang
1901	19 Feb 1901 – 7 Feb 1902	Ox	Metal	– Yin
1902	8 Feb 1902 – 28 Jan 1903	Tiger	Water	+ Yang
1903	29 Jan 1903 – 15 Feb 1904	Rabbit	Water	– Yin
1904	16 Feb 1904 – 3 Feb 1905	Dragon	Wood	+ Yang
1905	4 Feb 1905 – 24 Jan 1906	Snake	Wood	– Yin
1906	25 Jan 1906 – 12 Feb 1907	Horse	Fire	+ Yang
1907	13 Feb 1907 – 1 Feb 1908	Sheep	Fire	– Yin
1908	2 Feb 1908 – 21 Jan 1909	Monkey	Earth	+ Yang
1909	22 Jan 1909 – 9 Feb 1910	Rooster	Earth	– Yin
1910	10 Feb 1910 – 29 Jan 1911	Dog	Metal	+ Yang
1911	30 Jan 1911 – 17 Feb 1912	Pig	Metal	– Yin
1912	18 Feb 1912 – 5 Feb 1913	Rat	Water	+ Yang
1913	6 Feb 1913 – 25 Jan 1914	Ox	Water	– Yin
1914	26 Jan 1914 – 13 Feb 1915	Tiger	Wood	+ Yang
1915	14 Feb 1915 – 2 Feb 1916	Rabbit	Wood	– Yin
1916	3 Feb 1916 – 22 Jan 1917	Dragon	Fire	+ Yang
1917	23 Jan 1917 – 10 Feb 1918	Snake	Fire	– Yin
1918	11 Feb 1918 – 31 Jan 1919	Horse	Earth	+ Yang
1919	1 Feb 1919 – 19 Feb 1920	Sheep	Earth	– Yin
1920	20 Feb 1920 – 7 Feb 1921	Monkey	Metal	+ Yang
1921	8 Feb 1921 – 27 Jan 1922	Rooster	Metal	– Yin
1922	28 Jan 1922 – 15 Feb 1923	Dog	Water	+ Yang
1923	16 Feb 1923 – 4 Feb 1924	Pig	Water	– Yin
1924	5 Feb 1924 – 24 Jan 1925	Rat	Wood	+ Yang
1925	25 Jan 1925 – 12 Feb 1926	Ox	Wood	– Yin
1926	13 Feb 1926 – 1 Feb 1927	Tiger	Fire	+ Yang
1927	2 Feb 1927 – 22 Jan 1928	Rabbit	Fire	– Yin
1928	23 Jan 1928 – 9 Feb 1929	Dragon	Earth	+ Yang
1929	10 Feb 1929 – 29 Jan 1930	Snake	Earth	– Yin
1930	30 Jan 1930 – 16 Feb 1931	Horse	Metal	+ Yang
1931	17 Feb 1931 – 5 Feb 1932	Sheep	Metal	– Yin
1932	6 Feb 1932 – 25 Jan 1933	Monkey	Water	+ Yang
1933	26 Jan 1933 – 13 Feb 1934	Rooster	Water	– Yin
1934	14 Feb 1934 – 3 Feb 1935	Dog	Wood	+ Yang
1935	4 Feb 1935 – 23 Jan 1936	Pig	Wood	– Yin

犬

12

Year	From – To		Animal sign	Element	Aspect	
1936	24 Jan 1936 – 10 Feb 1937		Rat	Fire	+	Yang
1937	11 Feb 1937 – 30 Jan 1938		Ox	Fire	–	Yin
1938	31 Jan 1938 – 18 Feb 1939		Tiger	Earth	+	Yang
1939	19 Feb 1939 – 7 Feb 1940		Rabbit	Earth	–	Yin
1940	8 Feb 1940 – 26 Jan 1941		Dragon	Metal	+	Yang
1941	27 Jan 1941 – 14 Feb 1942		Snake	Metal	–	Yin
1942	15 Feb 1942 – 4 Feb 1943		Horse	Water	+	Yang
1943	5 Feb 1943 – 24 Jan 1944		Sheep	Water	–	Yin
1944	25 Jan 1944 – 12 Feb 1945		Monkey	Wood	+	Yang
1945	13 Feb 1945 – 1 Feb 1946		Rooster	Wood	–	Yin
1946	2 Feb 1946 – 21 Jan 1947		Dog	Fire	+	Yang
1947	22 Jan 1947 – 9 Feb 1948		Pig	Fire	–	Yin
1948	10 Feb 1948 – 28 Jan 1949		Rat	Earth	+	Yang
1949	29 Jan 1949 – 16 Feb 1950		Ox	Earth	–	Yin
1950	17 Feb 1950 – 5 Feb 1951		Tiger	Metal	+	Yang
1951	6 Feb 1951 – 26 Jan 1952		Rabbit	Metal	–	Yin
1952	27 Jan 1952 – 13 Feb 1953		Dragon	Water	+	Yang
1953	14 Feb 1953 – 2 Feb 1954		Snake	Water	–	Yin
1954	3 Feb 1954 – 23 Jan 1955		Horse	Wood	+	Yang
1955	24 Jan 1955 – 11 Feb 1956		Sheep	Wood	–	Yin
1956	12 Feb 1956 – 30 Jan 1957		Monkey	Fire	+	Yang
1957	31 Jan 1957 – 17 Feb 1958		Rooster	Fire	–	Yin
1958	18 Feb 1958 – 7 Feb 1959		Dog	Earth	+	Yang
1959	8 Feb 1959 – 27 Jan 1960		Pig	Earth	–	Yin
1960	28 Jan 1960 – 14 Feb 1961		Rat	Metal	+	Yang
1961	15 Feb 1961 – 4 Feb 1962		Ox	Metal	–	Yin
1962	5 Feb 1962 – 24 Jan 1963		Tiger	Water	+	Yang
1963	25 Jan 1963 – 12 Feb 1964		Rabbit	Water	–	Yin
1964	13 Feb 1964 – 1 Feb 1965		Dragon	Wood	+	Yang
1965	2 Feb 1965 – 20 Jan 1966		Snake	Wood	–	Yin
1966	21 Jan 1966 – 8 Feb 1967		Horse	Fire	+	Yang
1967	9 Feb 1967 – 29 Jan 1968		Sheep	Fire	–	Yin
1968	30 Jan 1968 – 16 Feb 1969		Monkey	Earth	+	Yang
1969	17 Feb 1969 – 5 Feb 1970		Rooster	Earth	–	Yin
1970	6 Feb 1970 – 26 Jan 1971		Dog	Metal	+	Yang
1971	27 Jan 1971 – 15 Jan 1972		Pig	Metal	–	Yin

犬

13

Year	From – To		Animal sign	Element	Aspect	
1972	16 Jan 1972 – 2 Feb 1973		Rat	Water	+	Yang
1973	3 Feb 1973 – 22 Jan 1974		Ox	Water	–	Yin
1974	23 Jan 1974 – 10 Feb 1975		Tiger	Wood	+	Yang
1975	11 Feb 1975 – 30 Jan 1976		Rabbit	Wood	–	Yin
1976	31 Jan 1976 17 Feb 1977		Dragon	Fire	+	Yang
1977	18 Feb 1977 – 6 Feb 1978		Snake	Fire	–	Yin
1978	7 Feb 1978 – 27 Jan 1979		Horse	Earth	+	Yang
1979	28 Jan 1979 – 15 Feb 1980		Sheep	Earth	–	Yin
1980	16 Jan 1980 – 4 Feb 1981		Monkey	Metal	+	Yang
1981	5 Feb 1981 – 24 Jan 1982		Rooster	Metal	–	Yin
1982	25 Jan 1982 – 12 Feb 1983		Dog	Water	+	Yang
1983	13 Feb 1983 – 1 Feb 1984		Pig	Water	–	Yin
1984	2 Feb 1984 – 19 Feb 1985		Rat	Wood	+	Yang
1985	20 Feb 1985 – 8 Feb 1986		Ox	Wood	–	Yin
1986	9 Feb 1986 – 28 Jan 1987		Tiger	Fire	+	Yang
1987	29 Jan 1987 – 16 Feb 1988		Rabbit	Fire	–	Yin
1988	17 Feb 1988 – 5 Feb 1989		Dragon	Earth	+	Yang
1989	6 Feb 1989 – 26 Jan 1990		Snake	Earth	–	Yin
1990	27 Jan 1990 – 14 Feb 1991		Horse	Metal	+	Yang
1991	15 Feb 1991 – 3 Feb 1992		Sheep	Metal	–	Yin
1992	4 Feb 1992 – 22 Jan 1993		Monkey	Water	+	Yang
1993	23 Jan 1993 – 9 Feb 1994		Rooster	Water	–	Yin
1994	10 Feb 1994 – 30 Jan 1995		Dog	Wood	+	Yang
1995	31 Jan 1995 – 18 Feb 1996		Pig	Wood	–	Yin
1996	19 Feb 1996 – 7 Feb 1997		Rat	Fire	+	Yang
1997	8 Feb 1997 – 27 Jan 1998		Ox	Fire	–	Yin
1998	28 Jan 1998 – 15 Feb 1999		Tiger	Earth	+	Yang
1999	16 Feb 1999 – 4 Feb 2000		Rabbit	Earth	–	Yin
2000	5 Feb 2000 – 23 Jan 2001		Dragon	Metal	+	Yang
2001	24 Jan 2001 – 11 Feb 2002		Snake	Metal	–	Yin
2002	12 Feb 2002 – 31 Jan 2003		Horse	Water	+	Yang
2003	1 Feb 2003 – 21 Jan 2004		Sheep	Water	–	Yin
2004	22 Jan 2004 – 8 Feb 2005		Monkey	Wood	+	Yang
2005	9 Feb 2005 – 28 Jan 2006		Rooster	Wood	–	Yin
2006	29 Jan 2006 – 17 Feb 2007		Dog	Fire	+	Yang
2007	18 Feb 2007 – 6 Feb 2008		Pig	Fire	–	Yin

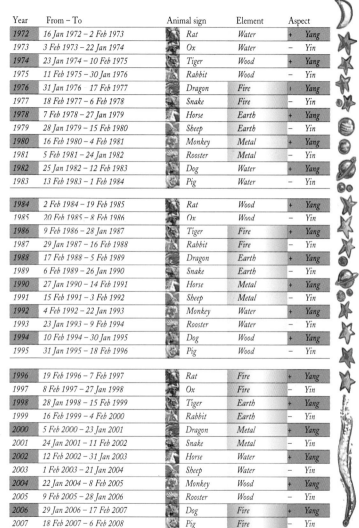

14

Introducing the Animals

THE RAT	♥ ♥ ♥ DRAGON, MONKEY	✖ HORSE

Outwardly cool, Rats are passionate lovers with depths of feeling that others don't often recognize. Rats are very self-controlled.

THE OX	♥ ♥ ♥ SNAKE, ROOSTER	✖ SHEEP

Not necessarily the most romantic of the signs, Ox people make steadfast lovers as well as faithful, affectionate partners.

THE TIGER	♥ ♥ ♥ HORSE, DOG	✖ MONKEY

Passionate and sensual, Tigers are exciting lovers. Flirty when young, once committed they make stable partners and keep their sexual allure.

THE RABBIT	♥ ♥ ♥ SHEEP, PIG	✖ ROOSTER

Gentle, emotional and sentimental, Rabbits make sensitive lovers. They are shrewd and seek a partner who offers security.

THE DRAGON	♥ ♥ ♥ RAT, MONKEY	✖ DOG

Dragon folk get as much stimulation from mind-touch as they do through sex. A partner on the same wave-length is essential.

THE SNAKE	♥ ♥ ♥ OX, ROOSTER	✖ PIG

Deeply passionate, strongly sexed but not aggressive, snakes are attracted to elegant, refined partners. But they are deeply jealous and possessive.

♥ ♥ ♥ COMPATIBLE ✖ INCOMPATIBLE

THE HORSE	♥ ♥ ♥ TIGER, DOG	✖ RAT

For horse-born folk love is blind. In losing their hearts, they lose their heads and make several mistakes before finding the right partner.

THE SHEEP	♥ ♥ ♥ RABBIT, PIG	✖ OX

Sheep-born people are made for marriage. Domesticated home-lovers, they find emotional satisfaction with a partner who provides security.

THE MONKEY	♥ ♥ ♥ DRAGON, RAT	✖ TIGER

Clever and witty, Monkeys need partners who will keep them stimulated. Forget the 9 to 5 routine, these people need *pizzazz*.

THE ROOSTER	♥ ♥ ♥ OX, SNAKE	✖ RABBIT

The Rooster's stylish good looks guarantee they will attract many suitors. They are level-headed and approach relationships coolly.

THE DOG	♥ ♥ ♥ TIGER, HORSE	✖ DRAGON

A loving, stable relationship is an essential component in the lives of Dogs. Once they have found their mate, they remain faithful for life.

THE PIG	♥ ♥ ♥ RABBIT, SHEEP	✖ SNAKE

These are sensual hedonists who enjoy lingering love-making between satin sheets. Caviar and champagne go down very nicely too.

15

犬

16

The Dog Personality

CARING, UNSELFISH AND ALTRUISTIC, you're one of life's givers. You've always got a kind word to say, an encouraging remark to offer, a reasssuring smile. You make time for other people, listen to their problems, provide a shoulder for them to cry on, lend them support and find some wise counsel from that seemingly bottomless well of common-sense philosophy that you possess. Your detractors, though, might say you're just a nosy-parker, giving advice when you've not been asked for it.

DOG FACTS

Eleventh in order ★ Chinese name – Gou ★ Sign of fidelity ★ Hour – 7PM – 8 .59PM ★ Month – October ★ ★ Western counterpart – Libra ★

CHARACTERISTICS

♥ *Reliability* ♥ *Perseverance* ♥ *Devotion* ♥ *Resourcefulness* ♥ *Unselfishness* ♥ *Honesty*

✖ *Introversion* ✖ *Nosiness* ✖ *Cantankerousness* ✖ *Anxiety* ✖ *Pessimism* ✖ *Cynicism*

Generous to strangers and devoted to his family, the Dog has a stout heart and an honest soul.

FAMILY TREASURE

There are times when, because you think you know best, you can be high-handed, marching in and taking over the whole shooting match. Such occasions are rare and more often your generosity of spirit and genuine concern come through. For where you're concerned, it's people that count. Money, power, prestige – none of them matter a fig to you if you don't have love in your life. Your family and loved ones constitute all the treasure you need.

Dogs know that the real treasure in life cannot be bought with mere money.

PILLARS OF SOCIETY

Disarmingly honest, highly principled and morally upright, those who come to know you soon learn to respect your integrity and value your friendship. With such sterling virtues, is it any wonder that Dog-born individuals sooner or later become recognized as pillars of society?

犬

18

Your Hour of Birth

WHILE YOUR YEAR OF BIRTH describes your fundamental character, the Animal governing the actual hour in which you were born describes your outer temperament, how people see you or the picture you present to the outside world. Note that each Animal rules over two consecutive hours. Also note that these are GMT standard times and that adjustments need to be made if you were born during Summer or daylight saving time.

11PM – 12.59AM ★ RAT

 Pleasant, sociable, easy to get on with. An active, confident, busy person – and a bit of a busybody to boot.

1AM – 2.59AM ★ OX

 Level-headed and down-to-earth, you come across as knowledgeable and reliable – sometimes, though, a bit biased.

3AM – 4.59AM ★ TIGER

 Enthusiastic and self-assured, people see you as a strong and positive personality – at times a little over-exuberant.

5AM – 6.59AM ★ RABBIT

 You're sensitive and shy and don't project your real self to the world. You feel you have to put on an act to please others.

7AM – 8.59AM ★ DRAGON

 Independent and interesting, you present a picture of someone who is quite out of the ordinary.

9AM – 10.59AM ★ SNAKE

 You can be a bit difficult to fathom and, because you appear so controlled, people either take to you instantly, or not at all.

11AM – 12.59PM ★ HORSE

 Open, cheerful and happy-go-lucky is the picture you always put across to others. You're an extrovert and it generally shows.

1PM – 2.59PM ★ SHEEP

Your unassuming nature won't allow you to foist yourself upon others so people see you as quiet and retiring – but eminently sensible, though.

3PM – 4.59PM ★ MONKEY

Lively and talkative, that twinkle in your eye will guarantee you make friends wherever you go.

 5PM – 6.59PM ★ ROOSTER

There's something rather stylish in your approach that gives people an impression of elegance and glamour. But you don't suffer fools gladly.

7PM – 8.59PM ★ DOG

Some people see you as steady and reliable, others as quiet and graceful and others still as dull and unimaginative. It all depends who you're with at the time.

 9PM – 10.59PM ★ PIG

Your laid-back manner conceals a depth of interest and intelligence that doesn't always come through at first glance.

Your hour of birth describes your outer temperament.

20

*The Dog will
defend his
beloved from
the hurts of
the world.*

The Dog Lover

*Forming intimate sexual
relationships takes a long
time and many Dogs
either go in for very long
engagements or don't
settle down until late in
life. An odd paradox
this, because a loving,
secure partnership is
central to your scheme of
things. You are, first
and foremost, a
family-oriented
person, someone who
functions a good deal
better within a
relationship than on
your own.*

THERE'S AN INNATE SHYNESS about you that can get in the way of making friends. Perhaps it's because you need to know people well before you entrust them with your affections. Or perhaps it's a touch of suspiciousness, a fear of being hurt and let down. For you are sensitive and emotionally tender. You don't easily throw slights over your shoulder and consequently your wounds take a long time to heal.

SOUL-MATES

Having found your soul-mate you make a loyal and true companion. As a lover, you're kind and gentle. Helpful and supportive, you care tenderly for those you love and are always anxious to please. You stick by your partner, sharing all the highs and lows of life, defending and protecting him or her if need be with every fibre of your being.

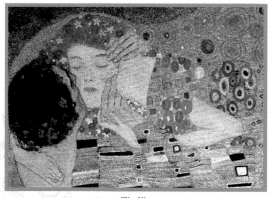

The Kiss
GUSTAV KLIMT 1862–1918

HONEST DOG

If you're contented and loved you're happy to plough your own furrow; you're undemanding and have simple needs. Because you find change disturbing, even if you're unhappy in love, you're still likely to stay put rather than casting off into the cold unknown. Honesty is your abiding principle, but harsh truths can do untold damage in a relationship and you need to learn to deliver your criticisms with tact if you are to avoid being accused of possessing a caustic tongue.

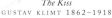

*Routine
does not
make a
Dog feel
dull.*

22

In Your Element

ALTHOUGH YOUR SIGN recurs every 12 years, each generation is slightly modified by one of 5 elements. If you were born under the Metal influence your character, emotions and behaviour would show significant variations from an individual born under one of the other elements. Check the Year Chart for your ruling element and discover what effects it has upon you.

THE METAL DOG ★ 1910 AND 1970

Uncompromisingly scrupulous and with extremely high standards, you have a serious outlook on life. Fiercely loyal, once you have shown your allegiance to a person, a party or a cause, there is very little that will persuade you to retract.

THE WATER DOG ★ 1922 AND 1982

With your keen insight, quiet contemplative nature and psychological penetration, you find it easy to appreciate other people's points of view. Your friendliness, warmth, tolerance and understanding guarantee you popularity amongst friends and colleagues alike.

犬

THE WOOD DOG ★ 1934 AND 1994

You're generous by nature and well-balanced by disposition. More adaptable but less independent than other Dogs, living and working within a large group is important to you as this gives you the sense of protection and support that is so necessary to your well-being.

THE FIRE DOG ★ 1946 AND 2006

You're a born leader with a charismatic personality. This element imparts dynamism – energy, enthusiasm, independence, a strong streak of adventurousness and bags and bags of charm. An out-going disposition and creative mentality ensure popularity and success.

THE EARTH DOG ★ 1958

Slow but sure, yours is a wise and kindly character. You have innate practicality, and invaluable talent when it comes to giving advice and dealing with money. Honesty, objectivity and impeccable integrity are your trade marks.

犬

24

*Rencontre
du Soir
(detail)*
THEOPHILE-
ALEXANDRE
STEINLEN
1859–1923

*The Dog and
the Horse
stand
shoulder to
shoulder.*

Partners in Love

THE CHINESE are very definite about which animals are compatible with each other and which are antagonistic. So find out if you're truly suited to your partner.

DOG + RAT
★ *Despite some dull moments, you can actually achieve a stable union together.*

DOG + OX
★ *You don't have much in common and are not truly comfortable with each other.*

DOG + TIGER
★ *Mutual respect and admiration make this a winning team.*

DOG + RABBIT
★ *Lots going for you here.*

Eiaha chipa
PAUL GAUGUIN 1848–1903

DOG + DRAGON
★ *A truly tempestuous affair that's not recommended for peace of mind.*

DOG + SNAKE
★ *Mutual attraction on sight.*

DOG + HORSE
★ *Tipped for lasting happiness, stability and success.*

LOVE PARTNERS AT A GLANCE

Dog with:	Tips on Togetherness	Compatibility
Rat	mutual respect	♥♥
Ox	odds against, but a glimmer of hope	♥♥
Tiger	solid!	♥♥♥♥
Rabbit	rock steady	♥♥♥
Dragon	keep walking if you want to stay healthy	♥
Snake	first comes the physical, then the mental	♥♥♥
Horse	you have what it takes	♥♥♥♥
Sheep	a clash of personalities	♥
Monkey	cheerful complementarity	♥♥♥
Rooster	difficult	♥♥
Dog	deep affection	♥♥♥♥
Pig	honest and sincere	♥♥♥

COMPATIBILITY RATINGS:
♥ *conflict*   ♥♥ *work at it*   ♥♥♥ *strong sexual attraction*   ♥♥♥♥ *heavenly!*

DOG + SHEEP
★ *A tiresome togetherness.*

DOG + MONKEY
★ *Not a bad shot this. With so much desire to pull together, you've got plenty going for you.*

DOG + ROOSTER
★ *Not a lot in common here, difficulties arise all the way.*

DOG + DOG
★ *Compassionate, understanding and harmonious, together you're likely to stay the distance.*

DOG + PIG
★ *A solid, amicable and honest partnership, even if a little unadventurous at times.*

The Dog and the Monkey find lust and love together.

26

Hot Dates

IF YOU'RE DATING someone for the first time, taking your partner out for a special occasion or simply wanting to re-ignite that flame of passion between you, it helps to understand what would please that person most.

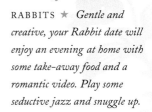

RATS ★ *Wine and dine him or take her to a party. Do something on impulse... go to the races or take a flight in a hot air balloon.*

OXEN ★ *Go for a drive in the country and drop in on a stately home. Visit an art gallery or antique shops. Then have an intimate dinner à deux.*

'So glad to see you...'
COCA-COLA 1945

TIGERS ★ *Tigers thrive on excitement so go clay-pigeon shooting, Formula One racing or challenge each other to a Quasar dual. A date at the theatre will put stars in your Tiger's eyes.*

RABBITS ★ *Gentle and creative, your Rabbit date will enjoy an evening at home with some take-away food and a romantic video. Play some seductive jazz and snuggle up.*

DRAGONS ★ *Mystery and magic will thrill your Dragon date. Take in a* son et lumière *show or go to a carnival. Or drive to the coast and sink your toes in the sand as the sun sets.*

SNAKES ★ *Don't do anything too active – these creatures like to take life sloooowly. Hire a row-boat for a long, lazy ride down the river. Give a soothing massage, then glide into a sensual jacuzzi together.*

犬

27

The Carnival
GASTON-DOIN 19/20TH CENTURY

HORSES ★ *Your zany Horse gets easily bored. Take her on a mind-spinning tour of the local attractions. Surprise him with tickets to a musical show. Whatever you do, keep them guessing.*

SHEEP ★ *These folk adore the Arts so visit a museum, gallery or poetry recital. Go to a concert, the ballet, or the opera.*

MONKEYS ★ *The fantastical appeals to this partner, so go to a fancy-dress party or a masked ball, a laser light show or a sci-fi movie.*

ROOSTERS ★ *Grand gestures will impress your Rooster. Escort her to a film première or him to a formal engagement. Dressing up will place this date in seventh heaven.*

DOGS ★ *A cosy dinner will please this most unassuming of partners more than any social occasion. Chatting and story telling will ensure a close understanding.*

PIGS ★ *Arrange a slap-up meal or a lively party, or cruise through the shopping mall. Shopping is one of this partner's favourite hobbies!*

Detail from
Chinese
Marriage
Ceremony
CHINESE
PAINTING

Year of Commitment

CAN THE YEAR in which you marry (or make a firm commitment to live together) have any influence upon your marital relationship or the life you and your partner forge together? According to the Orientals, it certainly can. Whether your marriage is fiery, gentle, productive, passionate, insular or sociable doesn't so much depend on your animal nature, as on the nature of the Animal in whose year you tied the knot.

IF YOU MARRY IN A YEAR OF THE...

RAT ★ *your marriage should succeed because ventures starting now attract long-term success. Materially, you won't want and life is full of friendship.*

Marriage Feast
CHINESE PAINTING

OX ★ *your relationship will be solid and tastes conventional. Diligence will be recognized and you'll be well respected.*

TIGER ★ *you'll need plenty of humour to ride out the storms. Marrying in the Year of the Tiger is not auspicious.*

RABBIT ★ *you're wedded under the emblem of lovers. It's auspicious for a happy, carefree relationship, as neither partner wants to rock the boat.*

DRAGON ★ *you're blessed. This year is highly auspicious for luck, happiness and success.*

SNAKE ★ *it's good for romance but sexual entanglements are rife. Your relationship may seem languid, but passions run deep.*

HORSE ★ *chances are you decided to marry on the spur of the moment as the Horse year encourages impetuous behaviour. Marriage now may be volatile.*

SHEEP ★ *your family and home are blessed but watch domestic spending. Money is very easily frittered away.*

Marriage Ceremony (detail)
CHINESE PAINTING

Marriage Ceremony
CHINESE PAINTING

MONKEY ★ *married life could be unconventional. As plans go awry your lives could be full of surprises.*

ROOSTER ★ *drama characterizes your married life. Your household will run like clockwork, but bickering could strain your relationship.*

DOG ★ *it's a truly fortunate year and you can expect domestic joy. Prepare for a large family as the Dog is the sign of fertility!*

PIG ★ *it's highly auspicious and there'll be plenty of fun. Watch out for indulgence and excess.*

YEAR
OF
COMMITMENT

犬

29

Detail from Chinese Marriage Ceremony
CHINESE PAINTING

犬

TYPICAL DOG PLEASURES

COLOUR PREFERENCES ★ *Pale yellow*

Cornelian

Jasper

Moonstone

GEMS AND STONES ★ *Moonstone, cornelian, jasper*

SUITABLE GIFTS ★ *Garden trough, rocking chair, puzzle, the latest novel, a massage session, silk flowers, lace tablecloth, red roses*

HOBBIES AND PASTIMES ★ *Gardening, craftwork, sailing, dancing, cooking, flower arranging*

Istanbul, a magnet for Dogs

HOLIDAY PREFERENCES
★ *A compulsive observer of human nature, you happily while away your time sitting at a café table in the street watching people go by. Choose Prague, Istanbul, Athens or Amsterdam.
You adore plants so why not visit some stately gardens?*

COUNTRIES LINKED WITH THE DOG
★ *Malta, Luxembourg, Korea*

The Dog Parent

犬

31

ONE OF THE MOST CARING, responsible and deeply devoted parents of all the Chinese Animals, Dogs always put their families first, and consider that putting others above their own offspring is tantamount to heresy. Staunchly loyal, you stick by and protect your children through thick and thin. When they're little, you do everything you can to make your home a happy, safe place in which your youngsters can grow and develop. You encourage them to learn at their own pace and find things out for themselves.

ALWAYS THERE

When your children choose their life direction, you wouldn't dream of standing in their way, but you let them know that you're rooting for them. And they know that you'll always be there for them if they're ever in need.

A dog will always keep a light in the window as a beacon for family and friends.

THE DOG HABITAT

The saying 'Cleanliness is next to Godliness' must have first been spoken by a Dog-born individual and applies specifically to your sign. You spend hours dusting and polishing your home, but although neat and orderly, there's always a comfortable feel about your environment. Deep sofas in attractive upholstery simply beg you to sit down and take it easy. You go for good taste so there's nothing showy about your house interior. Tradition is important to you so you're more likely to favour conservative styles and choose solid wood in preference to plastic, wool carpets before synthetics, antiques as opposed to contemporary furniture.

犬

Animal Babies

FOR SOME parents, their children's personalities harmonize perfectly with their own. Others find that no matter how much they may love their offspring they're just not on the same wavelength. Our children arrive with their characters already well formed and, according to Chinese philosophy, shaped by the influence of their Animal Year. So you should be mindful of the year in which you conceive.

BABIES BORN IN THE YEAR OF THE...

RAT ★ *love being cuddled. They keep on the go – so give them plenty of rest. Later they enjoy collecting things.*

OX ★ *are placid, solid and independent. If not left to their own devices they sulk.*

TIGER ★ *are happy and endearing. As children, they have irrepressible energy. Boys are sporty and girls tom-boys.*

RABBIT ★ *are sensitive and strongly bonded to their mother. They need stability to thrive.*

DRAGON ★ *are independent and imaginative from the start. Encourage any interest that will allow their talents to flourish.*

SNAKE ★ *have great charm. They are slow starters so may need help with school work. Teach them to express feelings.*

One Hundred Children Scroll
ANON, MING PERIOD

HORSE ★ *will burble away contentedly for hours. Talking starts early and they excel in languages.*

SHEEP ★ *are placid, well-behaved and respectful. They are family-oriented and never stray too far from home.*

MONKEY ★ *take an insatiable interest in everything. With agile minds they're quick to learn. They're good-humoured but mischievous!*

ROOSTER ★ *are sociable. Bright and vivacious, their strong adventurous streak best shows itself on a sports field.*

DOG ★ *are cute and cuddly. Easily pleased, they are content just pottering around the house amusing themselves for hours. Common sense is their greatest virtue.*

PIG ★ *are affectionate and friendly. Well-balanced, self-confident children, they're happy-go-lucky and laid-back. They are popular with friends.*

犬

34

A Dog pulls his weight in any team, whether leader of the pack or keen young pup.

Health, Wealth and Worldly Affairs

IT'S YOUR GENERAL philosophical acceptance of human nature and the vagaries of life that gives you resilience and keeps your health on an even keel. Because of this you have a remarkable ability to absorb and withstand the buffeting of events that life throws at you. Being happy is your best protection against disease; otherwise, a deep-seated uneasiness can bring out anxiety and problems associated with the nervous system.

CAREER

Insight and intuition play a strong part in your choice of

Because you like to please, you make a conscientious, loyal worker. A staunch believer in the status quo, you're in no hurry to change things. As far as you're concerned, if it works why tamper with the system?

occupation as well as in your day-to-day dealings with others. Cheerful and willing, you're thoughtful and helpful and, whether at the top or bottom of the ladder, you often take on extra responsibilities in order to lighten the loads of your colleagues. As a consequence, you're a popular and respected member of the workforce.

DOGS MAKE EXCELLENT:

★ Lawyers ★ Judges ★ Police officers ★ Teachers ★
★ Scientists ★ Nurses ★ Doctors ★ Surgeons ★
★ Carers ★ Welfare workers ★ Psychiatrists ★
★ Psychologists ★ Councillors ★ Politicians ★
★ Priests ★ Nuns ★ Clerics ★
★ Gardeners ★ Builders ★ Interior decorators ★

FINANCES

You're careful when it comes to money and, because you work hard, you know the value of spending moderately and wisely. Dog-born folk are invariably good at conserving their resources and many put a little money by on a regular basis to build up a nest egg and ensure against future adversity.

Intelligent and resourceful, what you lack in creative imagination, you make up for in practical, logical application. With your idealistic view of life, justice and fair-play are uppermost in your mind. So you're drawn to those occupations that deal with people who are underprivileged or work for the furtherance of human rights.

Dogs like to know that there is something for a rainy day in the family treasure chest.

FRIENDSHIPS

No-one could wish for a better friend than you. Honest and reliable, you take people as they come. You stand by your friends, sharing in their joy and sadness, providing advice and a strong arm to lean on.

East Meets West

COMBINE YOUR Oriental Animal sign with your Western Zodiac birth sign to form a deeper and richer understanding of your character and personality.

36

ARIES DOG

★ Your search for true spiritual rapport prevents you from settling down early on. When you do find your life partner you must learn that tact helps a relationship more than the brutal truth.

TAUREAN DOG

★ To a relationship you bring affection and fidelity. A pillar of the community, people feel reassured in your presence, but you're stubborn and like things done your way.

GEMINI DOG

★ Bright and intelligent, you could talk the hind leg off a donkey. Full of ideas, you're less intimidated by change than other Dogs. In love, you're charming and one of life's great romantics.

CANCERIAN DOG

★ Sensitive to people and places, you suffer from insecurity and need a loving mate to give you support. An instinctive home-maker, you're happiest when surrounded by your family.

LEONINE DOG

★ Proud and dignified, you appear self-assured; only someone close to you gets a glimpse of your self-doubts. A supportive partner is essential to boost morale.

VIRGO DOG

★ You take life terribly seriously, and are a born worrier. You work hard and dedicate yourself to those you love. Someone who can make you laugh would be an ideal mate.

37

LIBRAN DOG

★ Because you find it so difficult to make up your mind relationships seem to fall through your hands. Partners often fail to come up to your high expectations. Consequently, you're not likely to settle down until later in life.

SCORPIO DOG

★ Strong and passionate, you're a person of deep commitment. Once you've given your word, it is your bond. And that's how you like it to be in a relationship too – one hundred per cent loyal and true. Hell hath no fury like a Scorpio-Dog betrayed!

SAGITTARIAN DOG

★ Sincerity, warmth and generosity guarantee you a loyal following. More adventurous and fun-loving than most other Dogs, you like to look at life on a broad canvas. If you are hemmed in, whether mentally or physically, it does your health no good at all.

CAPRICORN DOG

★ You're the rock of ages – solid and enduring. A hard worker, you make a good provider, keeping home and accounts impeccably neat and tidy. As a partner you're caring and dutiful. However, you can be a mite prudish.

AQUARIAN DOG

★ Original and somewhat eccentric, you're one of the least materialistic people in the world. It's spiritual fulfillment that you seek, not wealth or fame. Caring for others is your mission in life and you dedicate yourself to anyone who is worse off than you.

PISCEAN DOG

★ Happiness for you centres around a quiet, restful environment, a loving home and a devoted partner. You're a peace-loving, sensitive soul, rather prone to over-anxiety. You dislike inbalance and therefore harmony and security are quintessential to your well-being.

THE
DOG

犬

38

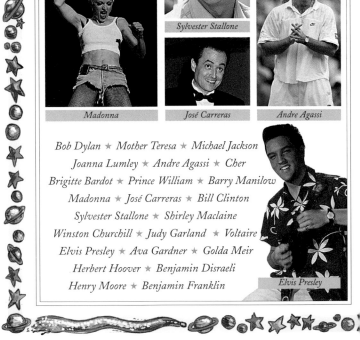

FAMOUS DOGS

Winston Churchill

Mother Teresa

Brigitte Bardot

Madonna

Sylvester Stallone

José Carreras

Andre Agassi

Bob Dylan ★ Mother Teresa ★ Michael Jackson
Joanna Lumley ★ Andre Agassi ★ Cher
Brigitte Bardot ★ Prince William ★ Barry Manilow
Madonna ★ José Carreras ★ Bill Clinton
Sylvester Stallone ★ Shirley Maclaine
Winston Churchill ★ Judy Garland ★ Voltaire
Elvis Presley ★ Ava Gardner ★ Golda Meir
Herbert Hoover ★ Benjamin Disraeli
Henry Moore ★ Benjamin Franklin

Elvis Presley

The Dog Year in Focus

IN DOG YEARS environmental issues and humanitarian schemes come to the forefront. Idealism, a key Dog concept associated with this sign, opens the way for grand philanthropic gestures. Conservation, animal welfare and civil liberties all come under the aegis of the Year of the Dog.

INTERNAL SECURITY

Politically, governments would be wise to review their defence budgets and to give greater priority to internal security. On the domestic front, the sign of the Dog is linked to property and we are advised to look after our personal effects and to upgrade our anti-intruder systems.

FAMILY FOCUS

The focus in this year is also on family life. Since Chinese philosophy tells us that marriage in the Year of the Dog brings happiness and good fortune, you would do well to tie the knot now.

ACTIVITIES ASSOCIATED WITH THE DOG YEAR

The discovery, invention, patenting, marketing, manufacturing or formation of: X-rays, the atomic bomb, the Iron Curtain, Xeroxing, the first Cannes Film Festival, tomb of Tutankhamen.

犬

Your Dog Fortunes
for the Next 12 Years

1996 MARKS THE BEGINNING of a new 12-year cycle in the Chinese calendar. How your relationships and worldly prospects fare will depend on the influence of each Animal year in turn.

1996 YEAR OF THE RAT — *19 Feb 1996 – 6 Feb 1997*

A prosperous, auspicious year for you in which you can make good progress and advance your aspirations. Though not a lover of change, any new schemes you initiate or new directions you take now will find favour and bring success.

YEAR TREND: EXPANSION HOLDS THE KEY

1997 YEAR OF THE OX — *7 Feb 1997 – 27 Jan 1998*

Leave new plans on the back burner, since pushing forwards in Oxen Years will only attract ill-will. Concentrate on matters closer to home and spend quality time with your nearest and dearest.

YEAR TREND: CULTIVATE YOUR GARDEN

1998 YEAR OF THE TIGER — *28 Jan 1998 – 15 Feb 1999*

Now's the time to give those new ideas an airing if you want them to reap their just rewards. Past efforts will be recognized by your superiors who will support you and facilitate your progress. You could meet your soul mate this year.

YEAR TREND: A BUSY TIME

犬

41

1999 YEAR OF THE RABBIT | *16 Feb 1999 – 4 Feb 2000*

Despite your penchant for the status quo, any fresh starts that you make in the Year of the Rabbit will ultimately prove successful. Whatever you do you'll find that luck and good fortune are on your side.

YEAR TREND: **AMBITIONS ARE FULFILLED**

2000 YEAR OF THE DRAGON | *5 Feb 2000 – 23 Jan 2001*

Dragon Years are never the easiest of times for Dogs. The dramatic nature of the year presents you with several hurdles that have to be negotiated and the atmosphere of tension brings out your anxieties. Best keep your head down and follow the pack.

YEAR TREND: **WATCH YOUR FINANCES**

Dogs work extra hard in the year of the Dragon.

2001 YEAR OF THE SNAKE | *24 Jan 2001 – 11 Feb 2002*

After the turmoil of last year, you'll find this a more favourable period, offering you plenty of opportunity to stabilize your position. Whilst at work your efforts will be recognized, spending more time at home with your family will bring deep contentment.

YEAR TREND: **SATISFYING**

THE
DOG

犬

42

2002 YEAR OF THE HORSE — *12 Feb 2002 – 31 Jan 2003*

With so much to do and so many places to visit, your feet will hardly touch the ground. You're in for a whirlwind of a time at work and at play and the emphasis will be on having fun.

YEAR TREND: AUSPICIOUS AND PROGRESSIVE

2003 YEAR OF THE SHEEP — *1 Feb 2003 – 21 Jan 2004*

In Sheep years the emphasis falls on home and family. Domestically, you are likely to encounter difficulties in that repairs to your house may cost you dear. A move is on the cards and this retrospectively will prove beneficial. Loved ones are supportive.

YEAR TREND: DIFFICULT BUT HEART-WARMING

2004 YEAR OF THE MONKEY — *22 Jan 2004 – 8 Feb 2005*

Last year's domestic problems rumble on and a change of residence becomes imminent. Nevertheless, you will make better progress now and by the end of 2004 you should find yourself in a stronger position both materially and occupationally. Your social life is buzzing.

YEAR TREND: KEEP A HIGH PROFILE

It's just one darned thing after another in the Year of the Rooster.

43

2005 YEAR OF THE ROOSTER *9 Feb 2005 – 28 Jan 2006*

Events occur thick and fast throughout 2005 and no sooner have you dealt with one crisis than another problem lands in your lap. But you also have some remarkably lucky breaks to even up the score, so accentuate the positive with these golden opportunities.

YEAR TREND: SWINGS AND ROUNDABOUTS

2006 YEAR OF THE DOG *29 Jan 2006 – 17 Feb 2007*

2006 promises to be an auspicious time when you can recoup the losses you have incurred in recent years. Whatever your ambitions, you'll find plenty of scope for attaining the recognition you deserve.

YEAR TREND: A TIME OF STEADY INCREASE

2007 YEAR OF THE PIG *18 Feb 2007 – 6 Feb 2008*

This year promises welcomed contentment. A legal, financial or health problem that's been hanging over you is soon resolved, giving way to a sense of peace and well-being. You feel you've now turned the corner and the future is looking rosy. Relationships bring joy.

YEAR TREND: A TIME TO RELAX